425

550

WINDOWS
ON·THE·WORLD

THE EARTH

·AND·HOW·IT·

· WORKS ·

Written by
Steve Parker

Illustrated by
Giuliano Fornari
Luciano Corbella

DORLING KINDERSLEY · LONDON

Editor Susan Berry
Art Editor Steven Wooster

Series Art Editor Roger Priddy
Series Editor Angela Wilkes
Managing Editor Vicky Davenport

Editorial Consultant Sue Rigby

First published in Great Britain in 1989
by Dorling Kindersley Publishers Limited,
9 Henrietta Street, London WC2 8PS

Reprinted 1990, 1993

Copyright © 1989 Dorling Kindersley
Limited, London

British Library Cataloguing in Publication Data

The Earth and how it works
  1. Earth – Juvenile literature
  I. Series
  550

ISBN 0-86318-333-6

Phototypeset by Southern Positives and Negatives (SPAN)
Reproduced in Singapore by Colourscan
Printed in Spain by Artes Graficas, Toledo S.A.
D.L.TO:1885-1992

CONTENTS

THE EARTH'S AMAZING LANDSCAPE

What is big and spectacular? A movie on the "big screen", perhaps? A rock concert with laser lighting at a stadium for 50,000 people? None of these man-made spectacles bears any comparison with the natural wonders of our planet, the Earth. The problem is that the Earth is so big, and its scenery so vast, that we have trouble picturing it. The facts about the Earth are just as hard to take in. The Earth is about 12,700 km in diameter: an excavator digging a hole at one metre per minute would take 24 years to reach the other side. The equator, around the middle of the Earth, is 40,075 km: at motorway speed (110 km per hour), it would take 15 days to drive around the Earth. The Earth's weight is almost 6,000 million, million, million tonnes. And its age, 4,600 million years, almost defies imagination. If the Earth had formed one year ago, all of recorded human history would be packed into the last minute.

Earth spectacular
These are just a few of the world's natural spectacles – most of them have been around for millions of years. But even a million years is a short time in the history of the Earth: equivalent to only two hours in one year. Nothing, not even giant rocks, lasts for ever.

Sacred rock
The Earth's largest single rock is Uluru (also known as Ayers Rock), in central Australia. Made of reddish stone, it measures 6 km long by 2 km wide, and is 348 metres high. It is a place sacred to the Aboriginals.

Chimney Rock
The 100-metre-high Chimney Rock, on the plains of Nebraska, USA, is visible 50 km away. The surrounding rock was worn down by rushing water over the past two million years.

"Frozen Waterfalls"
At Hamman-Meskoutine, Algeria, 10 hot-water springs bubble up, carrying many dissolved minerals. Over many centuries they have built a "frozen waterfall".

The Matterhorn
First climbed in 1865, Europe's Matterhorn (4,478 metres high) is one of the most famous mountains on Earth. A sharp pyramid, its sides have been gouged and shaped by glaciers for over two million years.

Guilin Karst
In Guilin, south China, there is a huge area of high, hump-backed limestone hills, 100 metres or more tall, separated by deep ravines.

Mount Fuji
A classic cone-shaped volcano, 3,776 metres high, Mount Fuji lies 110 km south-west of Tokyo, Japan. It has a crater 700 metres across at the summit, and a base 40 km wide.

Devil's Tower
In Wyoming, USA, Devil's Tower looms 265 metres above its surroundings. In Native American legend it was the home of an evil god. In fact it is a stump of hard rock pushed up 50 million years ago.

"Waterless Waves"
Long ridges of red sand, piled by the wind, look like giant waves in a waterless sea. This is the Arunta (Simpson) Desert, in central Australia. Some ridges are 30 metres high.

Urgup Cones
The Urgup Cones are a strange collection of small hills, some more than 30 metres high, in south-east Turkey. Caps of hard volcanic rock top some of the cones.

Las Marismas
"The Marshes" mark the mouth of the Guadalquivir River in south-west Spain. Coastal water currents have partly blocked the estuary to create a vast wetland of marshes, channels and islands.

5

Our changing Earth

Some mountain ranges and parts of the sea bed do not alter for millions of years. Yet whole areas of the Earth change in days, or less. In a few hours, two-thirds of the island of Krakatoa was blown to pieces in the biggest volcanic explosion in modern times. Shown here are a few glimpses of the immense power of nature.

Exploding island

In 1883, Krakatoa, an island between Sumatra and Java, erupted in a series of colossal volcanic explosions. The noise was heard 4,000 km away and tsunamis (seismic sea waves) 35 metres high killed 36,000 people. Krakatoa's volcano has since regrown.

Sheer ice

Icebergs the size of countries crack away from glaciers around the North and South Poles (pages 46–7). One measured 335 km long and 100 km wide – bigger than Belgium.

Lowest spot on Earth

The lowest land on our planet is the shores of the Dead Sea, 400 metres below sea level. The bed of the lake is the same distance again downwards. The salts in the water are about seven times more concentrated than in ordinary sea water.

6

All over in a flash
Around the Earth, lightning leaps from thunderclouds to the ground and back again about 100 times each second. A powerful bolt of lightning may be 6 km long, containing enough electrical energy to supply a large town for more than a year.

Building with stone
Across the shallow tropical seas of the world, tiny coral animals are busy building huge rocky reefs of limestone (pages 50–51). The Great Barrier Reef, on Australia's north-east coast, is 2,000 km long and covers an area four-fifths the size of the UK.

Sculpted by the sea
Each year, the waves of the English Channel cut away the cliffs in northern France. In living memory the pattern of headlands, overhangs, archways and needles has changed several times as a result (pages 48–9).

THE EARTH IN SPACE

The Universe is made up of millions and millions of galaxies, each one flying through space at incredible speed, away from all the others. A galaxy is made up of millions of stars, from relatively small ones – "white dwarfs" – to the immense "supergiants". We know that in one particular galaxy there is an average-sized star, which has nine small planets going round and round it. On the third planet outwards from this star there are many different forms of life. One of them is reading these words. It is you. You are on planet Earth, orbiting the star we call the Sun, in an enormous galaxy named the Milky Way, which itself is almost lost in a Universe so vast we do not know what its limits are.

The Sun and the nine planets orbiting it are called the Solar System. The planets are very different from each other, and it is doubtful that any one of them, except Earth, has life on it. But the chances are that, with so many millions of other stars, there may well be planets that resemble Earth in other galaxies, some perhaps with life like ours.

How the Solar System began

Hundreds of years ago, people did not know that the Earth was shaped like a ball. They assumed that it was flat, and that the stars circled overhead. They thought that at the edges of the Earth the seas poured into darkness, where monsters lurked. But in 1543 a Polish astronomer, Nicolaus Copernicus, had the idea that the Earth went around the Sun, and modern astronomy was born. One explanation of how the Solar System began is that a passing star pulled a huge stream or "tide" of matter from the Sun, and that this gradually united to form the planets. A more likely theory is that the Solar System formed from a vast cloud of gas and dust pulled together by the force of gravity (see page 12).

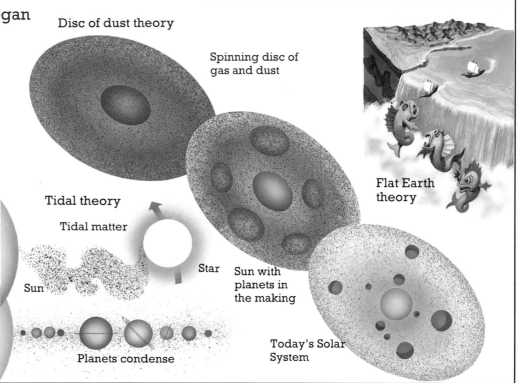

Disc of dust theory

Spinning disc of gas and dust

Flat Earth theory

Tidal theory

Tidal matter

Sun

Star

Sun with planets in the making

Planets condense

Today's Solar System

Journey from the Sun

Modern telescopes allow scientists to take clear, close-up photographs of the planets nearest to us. They record X-rays, radio and other waves as well as light waves. Spacecraft have landed on the two planets closest to Earth – Mars and Venus – and taken photographs and samples. Other deep-space probes have flown past the seven inner planets, with cameras clicking, so we now know much more about our neighbours in the Solar System.

Solar flare, thousands of kilometres long

Sun

The Sun

The Sun is a burning ball of gases, mainly hydrogen plus a little helium. It is 1,390,000 km across – more than a hundred times the diameter of the Earth. The surface temperature is around 6,000°C – hot enough to burn us even though it's millions of kilometres away.

Mercury

This innermost and hottest planet in the system is 4,880 km across. Only 58 million km from the Sun, its surface temperatures reach 350°C. It takes 88 Earth days to go around the Sun.

Mercury

Asteroids

Which planet is biggest?
The planets here
are shown with
their relative
sizes.

Jupiter

Neptune

Saturn

Uranus

Earth

Venus

Pluto

Mercury

Mars

Asteroids
In the great gap between
Mars and Jupiter are
swarms of tiny planets
called *asteroids*. Scientists
think they may be pieces
of a broken planet, or
(more likely) that they
were formed with the Solar
System and never became
planet size.

Earth
The third planet from the
Sun, 150 million km away
from it, Earth is 12,750 km
across. It takes 365 days
(our calendar year) for the
Earth to orbit the Sun. It is
the only planet with water,
and its surface gases are
mainly nitrogen and the
oxygen which is vital for
life. Surface temperatures
vary from −89°C to more
than 58°C, but the average
is a comfortable 20°C.

Earth

Venus
At 12,000 km across, Venus
is much the same size as
Earth and has a similar
structure. It takes 225 Earth
days to orbit the Sun, at a
distance of 108 million km.
The surface of Venus is
shrouded in clouds of
carbon dioxide gas.

Venus

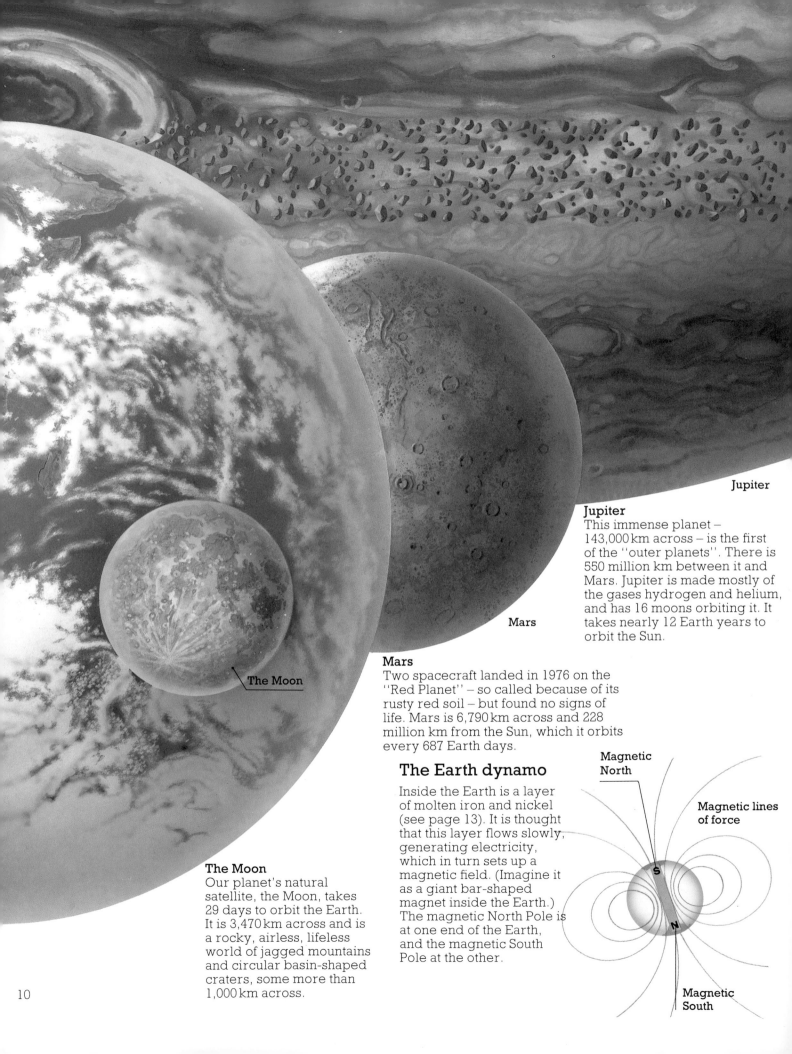

Jupiter

This immense planet – 143,000 km across – is the first of the "outer planets". There is 550 million km between it and Mars. Jupiter is made mostly of the gases hydrogen and helium, and has 16 moons orbiting it. It takes nearly 12 Earth years to orbit the Sun.

Mars

The Moon

Jupiter

Mars

Two spacecraft landed in 1976 on the "Red Planet" – so called because of its rusty red soil – but found no signs of life. Mars is 6,790 km across and 228 million km from the Sun, which it orbits every 687 Earth days.

The Earth dynamo

Inside the Earth is a layer of molten iron and nickel (see page 13). It is thought that this layer flows slowly, generating electricity, which in turn sets up a magnetic field. (Imagine it as a giant bar-shaped magnet inside the Earth.) The magnetic North Pole is at one end of the Earth, and the magnetic South Pole at the other.

Magnetic North

Magnetic lines of force

Magnetic South

The Moon

Our planet's natural satellite, the Moon, takes 29 days to orbit the Earth. It is 3,470 km across and is a rocky, airless, lifeless world of jagged mountains and circular basin-shaped craters, some more than 1,000 km across.

Asteroids

Neptune

Saturn
Like Jupiter, Saturn is a "gas giant", 120,000 km across and made mainly of hydrogen and helium. It takes 29 Earth years to orbit the Sun, at a distance of 1,427 million km. Its dazzling "rings" are probably made of swirling ice-covered rocks, some hand-sized, others as big as houses. The outer ring is 600,000 km across; each ring is only about 2 km thick!

Saturn

Uranus

Pluto

Uranus
2,875 million km from the Sun, and orbiting it once every 84 Earth years, is the ringed planet Uranus. It may have oceans 10,000 km deep beneath its surface clouds of gas.

Neptune
This planet is 49,500 km across, only 1,500 km smaller than Uranus. It takes 164 Earth years to orbit the Sun, which is almost 4,500 million km away.

Pluto
At the edge of the Solar System is Pluto, only about 3,000 km across. This icy, rocky world orbits the Sun every 248 Earth years, at an average distance of 5,900 million km.

Days and seasons
The Earth spins like a top, making one revolution every 24 hours, to give us night and day (right). It also goes around the Sun, once each year. But the Earth is also tilted by 23.5 degrees. This tilt gives us the seasons, because for six months of the year the upper (northern) part of the Earth leans towards the Sun, and so these months are warmer. Then the lower (southern) part leans towards the Sun, making it warmer there.

Earth

Night   Day

Sun   Moon

Spinning of Earth gives day and night

Earth's orbit around Sun

11

DOWN INTO THE CENTRE OF THE EARTH

Telescopes and spaceships have told us much about what is in the skies above our planet. But what is actually under our feet? What is our planet made of? Holes have been drilled far down in the Earth, but even the deepest of these reaches only 13 km below the surface – just about one-thousandth of the way through to the centre of the Earth. Fortunately, scientists can make good guesses about what is deep down inside our planet by studying *seismic* waves – the shock waves from earthquakes and underground explosions. Seismic waves travel at certain speeds and they are bent in specific ways according to the material they are travelling through. Seismic studies indicate that the Earth has four main layers: the crust on the outside, the mantle below this, then the outer core, and the inner core at the centre. Studies of Earth rocks, and also Moon rocks, as well as information about other planets, show that the whole Solar System formed at the same time. Our Earth is about 4,600 million years old.

You may wonder how it is that as the Earth spins round we do not fly off into space. The answer is the basic laws of physics that say that any object attracts or "pulls on" another object, and this force is called *gravity*. For most everyday objects gravity is too weak to be felt, but the enormous Earth exerts a strong pull of gravity and draws objects towards it, as Sir Isaac Newton realized in the 17th century when an apple fell on his head!

The atmosphere

Around the Earth is the *atmosphere* – the air we breathe – held by the force of gravity. It contains less and less oxygen the higher you go; above 150 km there is none. Climbers of very high mountains need oxygen tanks to breathe comfortably. The atmosphere is divided into four main layers (whose names end with "-sphere"), depending on the air temperature. Aeroplanes fly, and clouds occur, in the lowest layer.

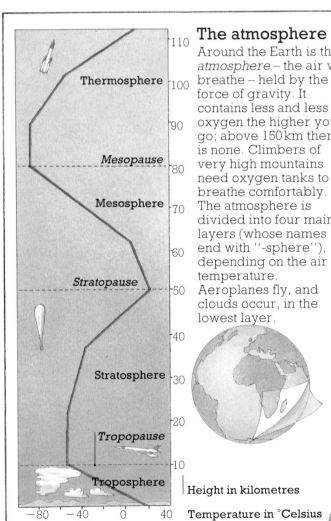

110
Thermosphere — 100
90
Mesopause — 80
Mesosphere — 70
60
Stratopause — 50
40
Stratosphere — 30
20
Tropopause
— 10
Troposphere

Height in kilometres

−80   −40   0   40   Temperature in °Celsius

The Earth – outside-in
Compared to the whole Earth, the rocks of the crust, which make up our continents and ocean floors, are thinner than the skin on an apple. If the Earth was a model about 25 metres across, as shown here, the crust would still be only a few centimetres thick. And the planet is not a perfect sphere. The diameter at the equator is 43 km greater than it is at the poles.

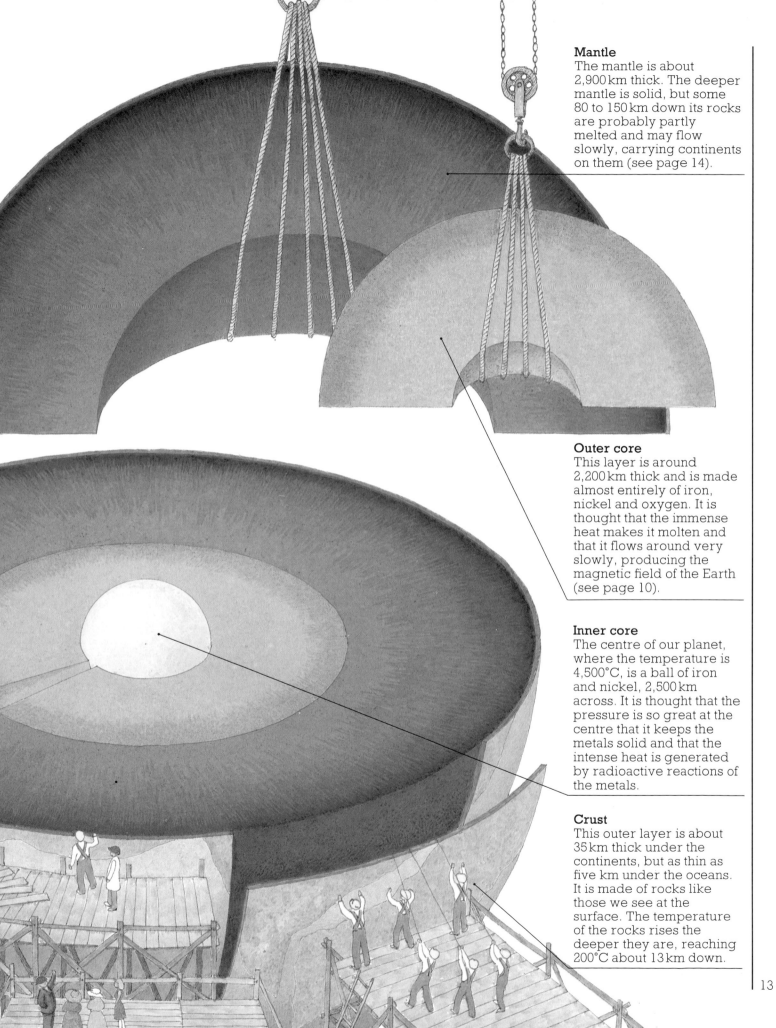

Mantle
The mantle is about 2,900 km thick. The deeper mantle is solid, but some 80 to 150 km down its rocks are probably partly melted and may flow slowly, carrying continents on them (see page 14).

Outer core
This layer is around 2,200 km thick and is made almost entirely of iron, nickel and oxygen. It is thought that the immense heat makes it molten and that it flows around very slowly, producing the magnetic field of the Earth (see page 10).

Inner core
The centre of our planet, where the temperature is 4,500°C, is a ball of iron and nickel, 2,500 km across. It is thought that the pressure is so great at the centre that it keeps the metals solid and that the intense heat is generated by radioactive reactions of the metals.

Crust
This outer layer is about 35 km thick under the continents, but as thin as five km under the oceans. It is made of rocks like those we see at the surface. The temperature of the rocks rises the deeper they are, reaching 200°C about 13 km down.

THE RESTLESS EARTH

The outside of the Earth is not one continuous piece, like the shell of an egg. It is split into seven giant, jagged-edged pieces called *lithospheric plates*. Each plate is curved (rather like a dinner plate) to fit the spherical shape of the Earth. There are also a dozen or so smaller plates – ''smaller'' meaning that they are only a few thousand kilometres across.

Each plate is made up of a thin portion of crust and a thicker portion of the outer mantle that lies beneath it (page 13). The seven two-layered plates together form a layer around the Earth called the *lithosphere*. Its average thickness is about 100 km. Rocks in the part of the mantle immediately below the lithosphere, called the *asthenosphere*, are at such high temperatures and pressures that they are partly melted, like sticky tar. So the lithosphere plates ''float'' on the asthenosphere. And float they do, because vast forces from within the Earth carry the plates very, very slowly around the globe in an ever-changing, ball-shaped jigsaw. Over millions of years the plates bump together, overlap and slide past each other, in the process making new areas of sea bed, building mountains, and causing volcanoes and earthquakes (see pages 20–25).

The making of island mountains

If you could make a slit about 200 km long in the Earth, somewhere near Japan, you might see a scene like the one below. The Pacific plate, moving in from the left, is gradually being forced under the Eurasian plate. The volcanic island chain of Japan marks their meeting. As the edge of the Pacific plate goes under it forms an oceanic trench 10 km below sea level. Some plates have only oceanic crust (like the Pacific plate), some carry only continental crust (see page 18), and some have both types.

Wandering continents

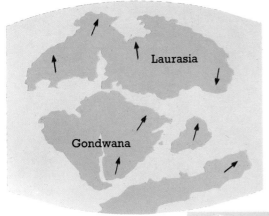

135 million years ago

Laurasia

Gondwana

65 million years ago

North America   Europe and Asia

Africa

South America   India

Antarctica

About 200 million years ago there was just one super-continent on Earth, called Pangaea. Slowly this split into two parts: Laurasia, which drifted north, and Gondwana, which went south. Gradually each of these split again until seven great land masses were formed. These *continents* have drifted by a few centimetres each year, and still do, to make the familiar map of the world we know today (see pages 62–3).

Eurasian plate

North American plate

Eurasian plate

Pacific plate

African plate

Australian plate

South American plate

Antarctic plate

——— Plates being made

——— Plates sliding past

——— Plates being destroyed

Melting in the mantle

As the oceanic part of the plate tilts under the continental plate, it causes earthquakes many kilometres down. Its rocks melt in the rising temperature of the mantle. This molten *magma* is under incredible pressure, and forces its way upwards through holes and cracks.

The world today, showing the main lithospheric plates

Pushing up islands
Magma, molten rock from deep in the crust, pours up through cracks to the surface and becomes *lava*, the molten rock coming out of a volcano. Repeated eruptions over millions of years gradually build a line of volcano-topped islands.

Going down
As the thin oceanic part of the Pacific plate moves towards the thicker continental plate, it is forced down into the mantle. This is the *subduction zone*. On the sea bed there is a deep trench, thousands of metres below sea level, where the oceanic plate disappears downwards.

Under the ocean
The oceanic crust is about 5 to 10 km thick; in the deepest oceans it is covered by the same depth again of water. The crust, on its plate, moves sideways about 1 to 2 cm each year – fast enough to be measured by modern scientific instruments.

At the edges of plates

Collision course
When two continental regions of plates come together, they are both too thick to be pushed back into the mantle. They collide, crack, fold and buckle to throw up great mountain ranges like the Himalayas (see page 16).

Growing apart
Where oceanic parts of two plates "meet", they are often pushed apart as magma wells up from the mantle, cools, and solidifies into basalt rocks that add to the edge of each plate. This is happening under the Atlantic Ocean (see page 18).

Sliding past
Another type of plate boundary is where two plates rub and slide sideways past each other. No new rocks are created or destroyed, but there is the occasional land-shattering earthquake (see page 20).

Roots of the mountain
Deep under mountains are vast chambers filled with solidified magma, called *batholiths*. The smallest cover 100 sq km. In time, when the mountains wear down, the batholiths may become exposed. They often contain valuable ores.

Crusts on the plates
Each lithospheric plate consists of a rigid piece of crust carried on a rigid piece of the outer mantle. The plates are about 70 to 80 km thick in oceanic areas, and 100 to 150 km thick in continental areas, giving an average thickness of 100 km.

MOUNTAINS IN THE MAKING

Around the world, mountains are being built as the edges of *lithospheric plates* ram into each other. And around the world, mountains are being worn down by snow, rain, wind and other natural forces. In general, younger mountain ranges like the Alps tend to have sharp peaks and deep valleys. Many millions of years of erosion round off the peaks, as in the Appalachian mountains in North America.

But plate movements are not the only mountain-builders. Volcanic eruptions (page 22) also make mountains. In fact the world's tallest peak, Mauna Kea, Hawaii, is 10,203 metres high, measured from the sea bed to the tip. Only 4,205 metres are above sea level. Other mountains are formed when an outcrop of hard rock is left after surrounding softer, usually sedimentary, rocks have been worn away.

Rocks on high
These mountains from across the world come in various shapes and sizes, reflecting the different ways in which they formed. The highest point on the Earth's surface is the summit of Mount Everest in the Himalayas, which towers 8,848 metres above sea level.

Earth's greatest mountains
The Himalayas have been formed in the last 45 million years as India, carried on the Australian lithospheric plate, collided with the Eurasian plate. The world's 20 highest mountains are in this and adjoining ranges.

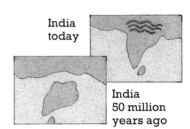

India today

India 50 million years ago

Young and ragged
The Alps of Europe are only a few million years old – a folded line of jagged mountains not yet worn and rounded by erosion. The range is 1,000 km long and the tallest peak is Mont Blanc, 4,807 metres high.

Dome of stone
About 300 million years ago a great lump of molten rock tried to force its way upwards from 3,000 metres below the surface. The overlying layers have since worn away. The ''lump'' is known as Stone Mountain, 251 metres high, in Georgia, USA.

Lichens

Folds and blocks

Two main mountain-building processes are block-faulting and folding. In the first, great cracks (*faults*) appear in the crust, and an enormous block of rock is pushed upwards as the plates on either side push together. In folding, two areas of crust push into each other and crumple up like paper.

Block pushed upwards

Fault (crack)

Fold mountain

Valley

Lammergeier

Mount Rundle

This mountain in New Zealand is a block-fault mountain formed when the central block of rock was forced up to form a large peak.

A natural frontier

The Zagros are a range of fold mountains along the Iran-Iraq border. On the thick limestone folds towards the southern end, there are towns and fields of crops. The northern area is still harsh and jagged.

Ibex

Chamois

Black grouse

Pine trees

Alpine marmot

Alpine hare

Alpine meadow flowers

Life on a mountain-top

Temperature falls and winds become stronger as you climb a mountain, and so life gets tougher. Mountain plants tend to be low-growing, with small, flat, hairy leaves that can resist wind and ice. Mountain animals have thick fur and are often darkly coloured, so that they absorb the Sun's weak rays. Many species migrate from the peaks to the foothills during the harsh winter.

17

THE OCEAN PROFILE

Oceans cover seven-tenths of our Earth. The largest is the Pacific, with a staggering area of 165 million sq km – about one-third of the globe. The ocean's surface may look almost flat, rippled only by waves, but under the water, the ocean floor is a fascinating landscape of flat plains, hills and jagged mountains. Sometimes tips of mountains rise above the water's surface as islands. There are around 25,000 of them in the Pacific alone.

North America

Continental crust
The rocks of the Earth's crust under the land masses – called continental crust – is thicker and has many more different layers than the crust under the Earth's oceans. The oceanic crust was formed more recently than the land – in the last 200 million years.

The Caribbean islands
The 300 islands of Bermuda are the limestone tips of mountains rising from the sea bed, 950 km west of North America. The main island, Bermuda Island, is 23 km long.

Like the rest of the Earth, the ocean floor is moving very slowly. An enormous 60,000-km-long chain of undersea mountains winds through the oceans of the world. Much of it follows the edges of the great lithospheric plates (page 14). It is here that the plates are moving apart in a process called *seafloor spreading*. As they slide apart sideways, molten rock (*magma*) from the mantle rises and cools and solidifies, adding to the edges of the plates. It is a region of volcanoes and earthquakes. The range in the Atlantic (the mid-Atlantic Ridge) is the greatest of all. Some chains of volcanic islands, such as those in Hawaii, form over "hot spots", or sources of radio-active heat in the mantle, far away from the plate edges. As the plates drift on, the older volcanoes are carried sideways and new ones are created to give a chain of peaks. The oceans are all formed since the break-up of Pangea. The Atlantic Ocean was formed in the last 100 million years.

At the bottom of the sea
The Atlantic Ocean covers one-fifth of the Earth. Under the sea is a central range of mountains with, on either side, higher peaks that break the surface and form islands, such as Bermuda and the Canaries. The deepest part of the Atlantic is the Puerto Rico Trench, near the Caribbean. (The mountains have been drawn taller than they are so that they can be seen more easily.)

Split in the sea bed
In the middle of the Mid-Atlantic Ridge is a deep trench called a *rift valley*. It is about 2km deep and 40km wide. This is the line along which molten rock rises from the magma and hardens, adding to the edges of the gigantic lithospheric plates as they move apart.

Grand Banks of Newfoundland

Close to the edge
Because of the sideways movements of the sea floor, the mountains towards the edges of the Atlantic are the oldest.

The Canaries
About 110km from the African coast are the seven main islands and several smaller islets of the Canaries. They are the peaks of undersea volcanoes.

Out in the middle
The Mid-Atlantic Ridge, 20,000km long, stretches along the middle of the ocean floor from Iceland almost to Antarctica. Crosswise cracks (*faults*) and underwater volcanoes make this range rugged and jagged. The sea here is about 2,700 metres deep.

North Africa

19

EARTHQUAKE!

How many earthquakes are there each year around the world? Perhaps 10? Possibly 50? In fact, there may be 100,000 or more, of which about 6,000 are detected by scientific instruments. Of course, most are either too small to do any damage or they occur in remote areas or under the sea. But about 1,000 cause some sort of damage, and 15 to 20 each year are strong enough to split the ground, topple trees and buildings, and cause great loss of life.

An earthquake is one of the most obvious signs of our restless Earth. Most earthquakes happen at the edges of the giant lithospheric plates (page 14) as these drift across the globe. Where two plates try to move past each other their jagged edges lock together until, suddenly, the strain is too much. The rocks slip and slide, the ground shakes and cracks, and there may be a deafening roar. Most earthquakes last only seconds or a few minutes. However their vibrations pass through rocks like ripples from a pebble thrown into a pond. These *seismic waves* travel through and around the Earth, reaching the other side in 20 minutes. Studying them has told us much about what is deep inside our planet (see page 12).

Earthquake damage

In a few places each year, earthquakes devastate buildings and gash open the ground. Holes and cracks several metres wide may open up and swallow cars and buildings. However these holes are quickly blocked by broken falling rocks, and they are rarely more than a few metres deep.

The wrong side of the street
On the far side of the road, there was hardly a tremble. A firm block of rock lies under here. On the near side, where the slippage and movement occurred, houses and shops were rattled and shaken apart as though made of toy building blocks.

Earthquake zones
The regions where most earthquakes happen closely follow the edges between the Earth's lithospheric plates (page 14). In many earthquakes, the point where most rock movement occurs, the *focus*, is deep below the ground. At the surface, above the focus, the damage is greatest.

(page 14)

The Richter scale
In 1935 the American earthquake expert, Charles Richter, invented a scale for measuring the strength of the vibrations from an earthquake. A measurement of 4 or more usually causes damage.

Force 1–2
Signs swing, slight trembling

Force 2–3
Liquids spill, definite tremors felt

Living on the fault line
The San Andreas Fault is the place where the Pacific and North American plates slide past each other. The San Francisco earthquake of 1906 was on this fault. Smaller earth movements happen, too; this row of trees has moved sideways from the rest of the orchard.

Force 4 Windows break, walls crack	**Force 5** Chimneys topple	**Force 6** Ground cracks	**Force 7–8** Major damage, railway lines bent

Built to last

People who live in areas where there are frequent earthquakes have learned to take various precautions. For example, some tall buildings are constructed in a pyramid or cone shape. This is a very rigid design, and with its stable, broad base, it is unlikely to topple over in an earthquake.

San Francisco's TransAmerica Building has a stable, tapered shape.

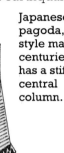

Japanese pagoda, a style many centuries old, has a stiff central column.

An uplifting experience

An earthquake not only shakes the ground, but may crack and tilt it as one side slips down (*subsides*) and the other pushes up (*uplifts*). A series of such cracks can create a new hillside in a few seconds. After the great Alaska earthquake of 1964, some parts of the land around Prince William Sound had subsided by 7 metres, while areas of the sea bed under the sound rose by more than 8 metres! This earthquake measured 8.3 on the Richter scale.

"Here is an earthquake warning . . ."

Predicting earthquakes is a tricky business, even with modern *seismometers* that detect the slightest tremors. Here are some earthquake-forecasting devices from ancient times. The Italian seismometer (*below left*), was invented in 1751. During a 'quake' the pendulum grooves the sand in the tray. This Chinese device (*below right*), dates from AD 132. A tremor causes the mouth of one of the dragons to open and a ball drops out.

Italian seismometer

Chinese dragon device

THE EXPLODING LANDSCAPE

Few sights on our Earth are more awesome than a volcano in action – the earth splits and molten red-hot rocks and ash spew out across the countryside. How does it happen? Deep under the Earth's surface is *magma* – rock at such great temperature that it has melted. In certain parts of the world, the solid rocks of the crust are thin and weak, and the magma presses on the rocks above. Imagine shaking a drinks can so the pressure builds up inside. When you pull off the tab, whoosh! A volcano is a bit like that. With colossal force, like that of thousands of tonnes of TNT, the magma bursts through the weakened rock to the surface. Its explosive exit into the open air is an *eruption* and it is now called *lava*. Once in the air, it quickly cools and becomes less runny, eventually turning into solid rock of the *igneous* type (page 26).

In some volcanoes, the lava flows from the opening (*vent*) and gradually hardens, piling layer upon layer. In others, the vent is plugged by hardened lava and the forces from below build up to many tonnes per square centimetre. At last the plug is blown out and molten rock is hurled high into the air.

When a volcano keeps erupting, we say it is *active*. When it has not erupted for many years, and all seems quiet, it is called *dormant* (''sleeping''). A very old volcano, which we are certain will never erupt again, is *extinct*.

Mountains made from molten rock
Depending on the minerals it contains, and the temperature and pressure of its formation, lava may be thick and viscous like tar, or thin and runny like engine oil. Often it has gas bubbles in it. The type of lava, and the force with which it erupts, and the amount of gas, all determine the shape of the volcano. Not all volcanoes are high cone-shaped mountains. They come in various shapes and sizes, as shown here. After thousands of years, when volcanoes are worn down, hills often form from the hard rocks which were once in the vent.

Volcano zones
There are about 500 active volcanoes on land, and many more under the sea (page 24). They are found mostly along the edges of the Earth's giant lithospheric plates.

Ex-volcano country
Formerly volcanic regions yield strange landscapes. Ship Rock Towers, New Mexico, is a 425-metre-high ''plug'' of solidified lava round the neck of a volcano. Le Puy, in France, is built on an extinct volcanic cone. Giant's Causeway, on Northern Ireland's coast, is a patchwork of six-sided columns formed when lava cooled quickly.

Le Puy

Ship Rock Towers

Spreading sideways
In a *flood basalt* or *shield* volcano, the lava is thin and runny. It wells up gently from a hole or crack and flows outwards to form gently sloping hills. In the vast flood basalts of Washington and Oregon, USA, some lavas flowed 150 km from their vents.

Giant's Causeway

Layers of lava
This is the popular picture of a volcano, cone-shaped with steep sides. Thick lava oozes out at intervals and there is an occasional explosive eruption of gas, cinders and lava.

Pile of ash and cinders
Ash-cone volcanoes tend to be small, with relatively little lava. Because the sides are not covered by erosion-resistant hardened lava, they wear down quickly.

Rocks from lava
There are dozens of types of rock made from cooled, solidified lava. Shown here are three forms: pumice, a light, frothy lava; obsidian, a natural, shiny black glass; and andesite, found in the Andes mountains of South America.

Pumice

Obsidian

Andesite

Volcanic "bombs" of molten lava.

In the cauldron
In the crater of an *effusive* volcano, molten lava churns and bubbles and sends up clouds of gas and steam. At intervals the lava wells up to run over the rim and add another patch to the volcano's slopes.

300–400°C

Vent

Lava 650°–1200°C

Ash and lava layers 250°C

Faults

Magma chamber 650–1200°C

23

Death of a mountain

Mount St Helens, in Washington, USA, lay dormant for 123 years. Then in May 1980 a volcanic eruption blew away one whole side of the mountain, reducing its height by 400 metres.

May 18, 1980

May 19, 1980

The biggest blasts

Volcanic eruptions such as Mount St Helens and Vesuvius (which destroyed Pompeii in AD 79) are small compared to the gigantic blasts of Tambora and Krakatoa (page 6).

Krakatoa

Tambora

Vesuvius

Mount St Helens

An island is born

Many islands, such as the Hawaiian group, are the tips of undersea volcanoes (page 18). In 1963 a new volcanic island appeared above the waves 10 km south-west of Iceland, near the Mid-Atlantic Ridge. It was christened Surtsey (the name of the Norse fire god). Within one month, scientists went ashore on the steaming lava to study the rocks. After three years, the main activity died down. Surtsey is now about 175 metres high; plants and animals thrive there.

Hawaiian island chain

Surtsey

Cloud of ash and hot gas, 500°C

Pumice raft

Underwater explosions

On the beds of the world's oceans, volcanoes erupt daily. Sometimes the lava explodes above the surface. It may contain bubbles of gas and solidify as a light "frothy" rock called pumice, that floats away in great rafts.

Ash rampart

650°–1200°C

Bubbling mud pots

In New Zealand, Iceland, Japan and other areas, natural hot-water springs mix with mineral particles and soil to form warm, bubbling mud.

Gushing geysers

In a geyser, water in an underground chamber is heated above its boiling point by molten rock (*magma*) lying close to the Earth's surface. As the pressure builds, the water and steam are finally forced through a hole. They spurt high into the air as a spectacular fountain, releasing the pressurized water and steam. The geyser then dies down, and the process starts again.

Geysers and fumaroles

In Icelandic, geysir means "gusher". And this is exactly what a geyser does – shooting hot water and steam high into the air. One of the world's most famous geysers is Old Faithful, in Yellowstone National Park, USA. It has been erupting every 30 to 90 minutes for more than a century. Each time it sends hot water 30–50 metres into the air, for up to 5 minutes.

Most geysers are in areas where volcanoes have been active in the past million years or so. The rocks under the surface are still very warm, and they heat rainwater that trickles through to the geyser's subterranean chamber. Most geysers spurt for a few minutes, then lie dormant for a time as the underground water is replenished and heated again. In a fumarole, or "fume hole", hot gases rather than water escape.

In New Zealand, Iceland, Japan and other places, geysers and hot springs provide a source of energy. In Reykjavik, the capital of Iceland, the central heating for the town is piped from the hot water geysers.

Fumarole

Superheated steam

Thick mosses

Fumarole

Hot spring

80°C

250°C
Water reservoir

Hot rocks

ROCK OF AGES

Our world is built on layers of rocks that have taken thousands of years to form. If you go down far enough below the Earth's surface, even in the middle of the ocean, you eventually come to rocks: hard substances made from minerals (see below). Their different types and proportions give each rock its particular character – colour, texture, hardness, and other features. There are three main types. Igneous ("fiery") rocks were first heated until they melted under the great temperatures and pressures within the Earth, after which they gradually cooled and solidified. Sedimentary rocks were laid down as layers of sand, silt and mud were squeezed together. Metamorphic ("changed") rocks were formed when temperature, pressure or chemicals changed the other two types of rock.

Common and colourful rock

You probably think all rocks look the same. They don't. Some are surprisingly colourful and some contain beautiful minerals (see page 56) that have become very precious. Shown on the right are some of the most common rocks – igneous, metamorphic and sedimentary – that make up our Earth's crust. Also included are rocks that are especially colourful, or useful.

Minerals make up rock

A mineral is a natural, non-living substance that has a characteristic chemical make-up. Different mixtures of minerals make the various types of rock. Granite, for example, a hard igneous rock, is made of three main minerals. The two most important ones are quartz (crystals of silicon and oxygen) and feldspar (silicon, oxygen and aluminium). The dark mineral is often mica.

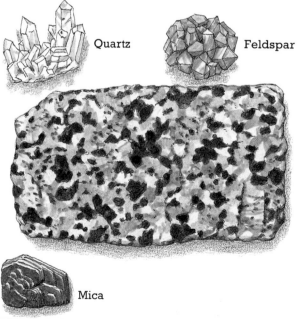

Quartz

Feldspar

Mica

Metamorphic rocks

Slate (*right*)

This dark, heavy rock, like many other metamorphic rocks, splits easily to form thin, flat, strong sheets. Slate is quarried and used for roofs and floors (and old-fashioned blackboards!).

Hornfels (*left*)

Hard, dense and often dark green, hornfels is made when certain sedimentary rocks are heated to 500°C under great pressure. They melt and then re-solidify into tiny crystals.

Gneiss (*right*)

A very commonly found rock, gneiss is usually formed in layers of different minerals: feldspar, quartz, garnet and mica. The proportions of the minerals determine its colour.

Mica schist (*left*)

This type of rock may peel into thin sheets, called mica, which is very resistant to electricity and hardly expands when heated. As a result it is useful for electrical and heat insulation. The glassy surface of mica gives a sparkle to the rock in which it is found.

Igneous rocks

Pegmatite (*left*)

A form of coarsely crystallized granite, it often contains very large crystals of quartz, feldspar and mica, sometimes metres long. Precious stones such as topaz (see page 57) are sometimes found in it.

Quartz porphyry (*right*)

A porphyry is a rock with large mineral crystals embedded in a mixture of tiny ones. Quartz porphyry also contains quartz crystals (page 56).

Sedimentary rocks

Fossil limestone
(formed from
living creatures)

Limestone (*above*)
There are many forms of
limestone, but they all
contain *calcium carbonate*.
Fossil limestone has shells
of animals embedded in it.

Oolitic limestone
(formed by
non-living
material)

Chalk (*above*)
This is a type of soft
limestone, made mostly
from tiny pieces of
microscopic shelled sea
plants.

Quartzite sandstone (*above*)
Unlike arkose, quartzite
sandstone is made almost
entirely of the mineral
quartz, which forms the
grains of ordinary beach
sand. The grains are 2 mm
to $\frac{1}{16}$ mm across.

Arkose sandstone (*above*)
Sandstones are made when
sand grains settle and are
squeezed together and
cemented by other mineral
crystals. Arkose sandstone
has a mixture of quartz and
feldspar minerals.

Tufa (*above*)
This soft, bubble-filled
rock is made up mainly of
calcite (calcium carbonate).
It is deposited from water
around hot springs.
Ancient Romans used tufa
for building.

Ironstone (*above*)
An ironstone is a rock that
contains iron. It can be
used as an *ore*, from which
the iron is extracted and
used to make metallic iron
and steel. Modern industry
depends on iron to make
steel for machines,
vehicles, bridges,
buildings . . .

Flint (*left*)
Prehistoric humans
chipped sharp-edged flints
to make the first tools, and
to make sparks for their
fires. It is a dark, dense,
hard rock that occurs in
rounded lumps.

Shale (*above*)
This is an abundant
sedimentary rock. Some
shales contain remains of
animals and plants. The oil
we use today comes from
shales (page 54).

The story of a rock
Chalk is a sedimentary rock
formed from particles settling
on the sea bed. Yet today, chalk
is found far from the sea. Why?
About 100 million years ago,
shallow seas covered much of
today's continents. Chalky
sediments settled in them.
Gradually, continents drifted
apart (page 14) and the chalk
was carried along. Buckling of
the land then lifted the chalk to
its present positions.

100 million years ago

50 million years ago

Today

27

THE RECORD IN THE ROCKS

The spectacular steep-sided valley, or gorge, known as the Grand Canyon, in north-western Arizona, USA, is one of the natural wonders of the world. Cut into the rocks over thousands of years by the waters of the Colorado River and by winds, it is 440 km long, and its width varies from about 6 to 30 km. In places, it is more than 1.5 km from top to bottom. A 169-km length of the canyon has been made a US National Park. But the gorge is more than just a spectacular cleft in the Earth's surface. As the river has cut its way downwards, it has exposed different layers of rocks that were formerly invisible under the surface. They are mostly sandstones and limestones (see page 27), sedimentary rocks formed when the area was covered by shallow seas, millions of years ago. As a result they contain many fossils of extinct sea creatures (see page 30). Going down the steep trails to the bottom of the gorge is like travelling back in time – the lower you go, the older the rocks.

Canyon of many colours
The layers of rocks in the Grand Canyon are of many colours – the different minerals they contain, like iron and copper, are not removed by weathering. There is little rain here, and the Colorado River is fed by rain falling way east, in the Rocky Mountains. The only plants are scrubby thorn bushes and a few juniper trees.

The young canyon
Thousands of years ago, the Colorado River was just beginning to gouge its way through the rock in a meandering course. Then the sea level lowered and the river gained more force, cutting vertically through the layers of rock.

The cliff tops
Rocks near the top of the cliffs are about 250 million years old. They contain fossils of reptiles, insects and fern fronds.

The steep wall
Halfway down the canyon, the limestones are about 400 million years old. The fossils here include fish with bony plates of armour. Further down, the fish disappear and the only traces of life are wiggly lines – perhaps trails of worms or shellfish in the ancient sea bed.

Rock pile
Near the bottom, the rocks are 2,000 million years old; they contain no traces of animal or plant life. Heaped on them are piles of broken stones and debris along the river banks. Many of these have been broken off the walls above by the action of wind, rain and ice.

River bed

The story of life

200 million years ago

400 million years ago

500 million years ago

The rock layers of the Grand Canyon are still flat and horizontal, roughly as they were laid down millions of years ago. Each layer contains a fossilized selection of the animals and plants alive when it was formed. The creatures above – found in the fossils – show the story of life in this area through the ages.

The river bed
The Colorado River is still cutting downwards, making the canyon ever deeper. Often the water is hidden by hanging mists. Sometimes the river floods and scours clean its banks.

PRESERVED IN STONE

Rocks can tell a fascinating story because they sometimes contain traces of once-living things that have been preserved as fossils – literally turned into stone. How did it happen? Many thousands of years ago an animal or plant died and sank to the bottom of a lake, river or sea. The soft parts of its body soon rotted away. But the hard parts, like bones, teeth or shells remained, and became covered as more sand or mud settled on top. Gradually water seeped into the bone or shell, carrying minerals that turned it into stone. As the layers of mud and sand are squashed down, the remains get buried deeper and deeper and the mud or sand eventually turns into the form of rock – known as sedimentary rock – in which the fossils are found.

Fossils from rocks of different ages, many, many hundreds of years apart, can be used to build up a picture – the "fossil record" – of how life on Earth has changed. The very earliest fossils in rocks more than 3,000 million years old are of microscopic blob-like creatures. Exactly what made them is not known. Rocks from 590 million years ago contain fossils of familiar-looking shellfish and other creatures. About 240 million years ago the fossils of the first dinosaurs appeared, but by 65 million years ago they had disappeared and fossils of mammals became more common.

Back to the beginning of life

Fossilized remains of animals and plants from millions of years ago are shown here. Because of the way the rocks in which they are found are formed, the fossils found in the lower layers are usually older than those in the upper layers. In recent years, the age of some rocks has been measured by detecting how much of a certain kind of radiation they contain. This radioactive dating *can determine the age of a rock within a few million years.*

Corals
The tiny creatures called corals build cup-shaped limestone skeletons (page 50) that form good fossils. Most reef-forming fossil corals date from about 230 million years ago.

Feathers and mats
Bryozoans (sea mats) were creatures that resembled corals, and formed net-like fossil traces in limestones from about 500 million years ago. The delicate, branching sea feathers are related to starfish and sea urchins.

Ammonites

The ammonites are one of the best-known fossil groups, partly because their strong curly-patterned shells fossilized well, and also because there were lots of them around 144 to 65 million years ago.

Fishes and starfishes

Even though starfish skeletons are brittle and easily broken, fossils show that these creatures lived more than 450 million years ago. Fossils of fish, the first animals with backbones, appeared about 500 million years ago. They became abundant between 408 and 360 million years ago. This time was called "The Age of Fishes".

Plants

The earliest land plants are known from fossils of 438 to 408 million years ago. Many prehistoric plants were giant tree-like ferns. They were very common about 360 to 286 million years ago.

Sea-snails and other shells

Shells fossilize well, and more than 15,000 different kinds of fossilized sea-snails have been discovered. Snails seem to have reached their greatest variety 55 to 38 million years ago.

Trilobites

These famous fossil creatures swarmed on the seabeds 505 to 438 million years ago. They are related to today's insects, spiders and crabs but by 200 million years ago they had virtually died out.

THE CHANGING WEATHER

What's the weather like today? Is it sunny, or cloudy, or raining? Perhaps even foggy or snowing? Our weather is constantly changing, both from place to place, and in the same place on different days. At this moment there may be rain in Rome, sun in San Francisco, and cloud in Calcutta.

But it is very unlikely to be snowing in the Sahara, or warm enough to sunbathe at the South Pole. Because, although the weather varies from day to day (and even from minute to minute), on a longer time scale it is more predictable. Different parts of the world have their own regular yearly weather patterns. We call the long-term pattern the *climate*.

What makes the weather change? The answer begins with the Sun. As the Earth spins round, the Sun's rays warm different parts of the atmosphere (see pages 8–11). Warmed air rises, and pushes cooler air to one side. This moving air is wind. As air rises, it cools and its *water vapour* condenses to form clouds and rain (see page 34). The Sun also controls average temperatures. Tropical areas are warm because the Sun's rays come down from directly overhead. They have little atmosphere to pass through, and so not much of their heat is absorbed. At the poles, the Sun's slanting rays pass through much more atmosphere. More of their heat is absorbed, and so at ground level the rays are not so warm.

Weather eye in the sky
About 1,000 km above the Earth, an orbiting satellite takes photographs of huge cloud banks and other weather features, and beams them down as radio signals to a receiving station on the ground. Here, computers create the "satellite picture" seen each day on TV. These satellites have helped weather experts to predict the weather more accurately.

Clear and sunny
Areas where there are no clouds must be having sunny weather! The Earth's surface is laid out like a giant map, with the mountains, lakes and coastlines clearly visible. The cameras on board modern satellites can take photographs in amazing detail. They can even make out shapes as small as a car.

Rain on the way
The tops of clouds look different from the undersides that we see from Earth. These dark clouds (*nimbostratus*) are a sign that it is raining beneath. In some areas of the tropics it always rains heavily for certain weeks of the year, a time called the *monsoon* season.

Blowing in the wind
The spinning of the Earth tends to make winds bend to the right in the northern half of the world, and to the left in the southern half. This is called the Coriolis effect. In some ocean areas at the equator, there may be no wind for weeks.

Thick, thick snow
If the temperature in a cloud is below 0°C, water vapour in it may turn into tiny ice crystals. These lump together to form snowflakes, which fall to the ground. At times, almost a quarter of the Earth's land surface is covered with snow.

Hurricane force
Hurricanes and typhoons – like whirlpools of very high winds – form mostly over warm tropical oceans. Winds of more than 120 km per hour revolve around a central "eye", where there is almost no wind at all.

Weather surveying satellite

WATER GOES ROUND AND ROUND

Water is everywhere, but not always visible. Did you know that it covers seven-tenths of the Earth's surface, as seas and oceans, and that two-thirds of your body is made up of water? The quantity of water on Earth is always the same, but the water itself moves about. The Sun's rays warm it and it apparently "dries" but it, in fact, turns into invisible water vapour that passes into the atmosphere in a process called evaporation. As the water vapour rises upwards, the air becomes cooler and turns back (*condenses*) into billions of tiny water droplets so light that they do not fall. Masses of these droplets form clouds. From time to time the droplets join together to make one drop of water. Too heavy to float, it falls back to Earth as a raindrop.

This sequence is called the water cycle and it is part of our weather. Clouds and rain, ice and snow are more common in some places than others. They have a great effect on what lives where, as you can find out on page 36.

Up in the clouds

Different types of clouds form at different heights, and each brings a certain kind of weather. Low, dark nimbostratus clouds mean rain. Huge, towering cumulonimbus clouds may bring thunderstorms. Some high mountains, like Everest, are often shrouded in clouds.

Cirrus

Altostratus

Cumulonimbus thunderclouds

Cumulus

Nimbostratus

Stratus

Water on the move

The Earth's water goes round unceasingly. Snow and rain fall to the ground and run as glaciers and rivers to the sea. Water from the land, sea, plants and animals passes back into the atmosphere as water vapour. You are part of this cycle. Your steamy breath on a cold morning is the vapour from your lungs condensing into water droplets.

1 Snow falling

In cold areas and over mountains, and in winter, the water often returns to the Earth's surface as snow. Eventually the Sun's rays meet the snow, and it runs into gutters, gulleys and streams and back into the ocean.

Snow falls on high ground

Evaporation from glaciers

Glaciers melt into ocean

2 Evaporation

Even on a cold day, the Sun's rays and the drying effect of wind encourage water to turn from liquid into water vapour in the air (*evaporate*). Water evaporates from rivers, lakes, glaciers, snowfields, and from city streets!

3 Rain, rain, go away

Rain occurs when moist winds from the sea blow over the land. Rain also comes from depressions (low pressure air systems) and from thunderclouds that form on hot summer days.

Rain falls on lower ground

Sun

6 Clouds on high
As the wind blows over mountains, the air rises and cools. The water vapour it carries condenses to form clouds. With more condensation, the water forms rain, snow, or hail – and its journey begins all over again.

Rainbow

Vapour rising and condensing

Forest

Evaporation from lakes and rivers

Lake

5 Fog and mist
Fogs and mists are like clouds at ground level. Water vapour condenses and collects on the ground as dew. If you go out in mist or fog beads of moisture collect on your clothes.

Transpiration from plants

Rivers flow into sea

Evaporation from sea

4 Transpiration
Plants take in water through their roots, pass it up their stems, and evaporate the moisture from their leaves as water vapour into the air. This process (called *trans-piration*) sends vast amounts of water into the atmosphere.

LIFE AROUND THE WORLD

Plants and animals live in nearly all parts of the world but the wildlife at the icy poles is completely different from that at the steamy, hot equator. Temperature and water are the keys to what lives where. The hotter and damper it is, within reason, the more plants and creatures there are, and the greater the variety. But many of the plants and animals around the world have adapted over millions of years to cope with very difficult conditions – polar animals have extra layers of fat to cope with the cold, for example.

As you travel north or south from the equator the average temperature gradually falls, because the Sun's rays are weakened by passing through more atmosphere (page 32). At the equator, the temperature is about 25° to 30°C every day – hotter than days in cool areas. Near the South Pole it may rise above freezing in midsummer, but the average is −50°C – far colder than your freezer. These ''bands'' of temperature around the Earth create different types of plant and animal life suited to the particular conditions. Because ocean currents and winds affect temperature, and because rainfall varies, the bands are not identical both sides of the equator.

Each region has its own climate (page 32) and particular animals that have adapted to it.

What grows where

An imaginary view from pole to equator (continued on pages 38–9) shows that the rising temperatures closer to the equator bring with them a greater variety of plants and animals. Each region is usually named after the plants that grow in greatest abundance, such as coniferous trees or grassland. This is because the plants that grow determine the type of animals that have adapted best to living there.

Snowline

Treeline

Iceberg

Polar bear

Seal

Penguin

Pack ice

Hardwood, broad-leaved trees:
beech, oak, elm

Magpie

Alpine tundra

Coniferous
trees

Grizzly bear

Fallow
deer

Reindeer

Badger

Fox

Moose

Mossy tundra

Temperate forest
The term "temperate"
describes the cool region of
the world. In its forests trees
like oaks and maples lose their
leaves in winter. Badgers,
foxes, martens, squirrels and
various types of deer live in
these woodlands.

Coniferous forest
South of the tundra are vast
tracts of evergreen, cone-
bearing trees called conifers,
whose needle-shaped leaves
withstand the freezing winters.

Tundra
Around the frozen Arctic are
the treeless lands called
tundra. They are ice-covered
in winter, but during the brief
summer, mosses and flowers
spring up, providing food for
reindeer, lemmings and other
creatures.

Lynx

Polar ice-cap
At the ends of the Earth, life-giving
fresh water is frozen solid. So there
are no land plants. Only the surface of
the sea freezes, underneath are tiny
floating plankton or fish, providing
food for a few large creatures that can
live in or near the water. These
include polar bears (from the Arctic)
and penguins (from the Antarctic).

Polar ice-cap

Coniferous
forest

Temperate
forest

Grassland

Desert

Tropical forest

Tundra

37

Sand dune

Spider monkey

Camel

Cactus

Rattlesnake

Gila monster lizard

Tiger

Tapir

Kopjes (rocky outcrops)

Desert
Some deserts are hot, some are cold – but they are all very dry and barren. A desert is created when more water is lost by evaporation (see page 34) than falls as rain. Plants are few and far between, as only tough grasses, cacti and thorny bushes survive. Animals include lizards, desert mice and camels. About one third of the Earth's land surface is desert or semi-desert.

	Wheat		Rice
	Maize		Millet
	Potatoes		

Tropical forest
The hot, damp lands near the equator – the *tropical* forest – are the richest in wildlife of all the regions. There may be ten times as many kinds of plants in these Tarzan-like jungles, and a hundred times as many kinds of animals, as in an equal area of temperate forest. In fact, tropical forests contain two-fifths of all plant and animal species.

Grassland
Vast expanses of grassland occur in temperate and tropical regions, in areas where you do not get enough rainfall for forests to grow. They include the savannahs of Africa, the steppes of Asia, the prairies of North America and the pampas of South America.

Toucan

Hornbill

Gibbon

Lianas
and vines

Nature under the plough

If you compared our planet today with how it was 5,000 years ago, you would find there had been enormous changes. Vast tracts of land that were once "wild" have been turned over to farming or industry. The prairies of North America are still grasslands, but the original wild grasses (and the buffalo that grazed them) have all but disappeared. Today, these soils are ploughed and sown with wheat and other food crops. The temperate forests that once covered much of Europe have been cut down for timber to build ships, houses and furniture. In their place are fields of rice, barley, beet, potatoes and other food crops. The tropical forests, nature's richest storehouses, are being cut down for hardwood timber, for industries like paper-making, and to make way for farmlands and factories, at the rate of an area the size of New York City every four days.

Giraffe

Acacia tree

Zebra

Wildebeest

Rhinoceros

Lion

MAKING NEW LAND

Throughout the history of the Earth, there has been an endless battle between the land and the sea. It is still happening today. In some parts of the world, the sea is winning and the coastline is being eaten away (see page 48). But in other areas, as in the Mississippi Delta, shown here, land has the upper hand. Why is this?

As a river enters the sea, its waters flow less quickly. The tiny waterborne particles of sand, silt, mud and clay begin to sink, and then slowly settle. Sand and other relatively large particles settle first, near the shore. The smallest particles, such as clays, may be carried many kilometres out to sea before they sink. This settling out is called *sedimentation*, and the particles *sediments*. As they collect, they raise the sea bed. In certain conditions (see below) a strip of land forms around the river's mouth and advances into the sea, as more sediments add to it. This is a river *delta*, and it is land won from the sea. It has happened, for example, in Egypt at the mouth of the Nile, in India at the mouth of the Ganges and here at the mouth of the Mississippi; it can happen fast, too: the Mississippi Delta is growing by about 90 metres each year!

How a delta forms

Some deltas are delicate – the loose sediments can be washed away in a single storm. But coastal plants, such as mangrove trees and marram grass on sand dunes, help to make them more permanent. The plants grow into the shallow water, slowing down the flow of water, so more particles settle. Over hundreds of years, the loose sediments turn into firm, dry land. Eventually, they become sedimentary rock (see page 26).

Mangrove trees

Roots and stems slow water flow

Clay and smaller particles

Sand and larger particles

Marram grass on dunes

Roots bind particles together

More sediment collects

"Ol' Man River" and his delta

The great Mississippi River collects water from two-fifths of the USA's land area, and flows into the Gulf of Mexico near New Orleans. (Its name comes from an Algonquin Indian word for "Father of Waters".) Over hundreds of years, shifts in the river's course, as one channel silts up, have altered the position of the delta. In this aerial view, taken by satellite, the red areas show the land.

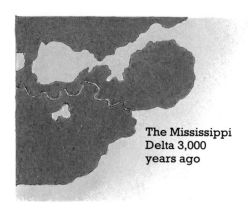

The Mississippi Delta 3,000 years ago

Satellite

Where the delta was
About 3,000 years ago, these islands marked the edge of the delta. But the ocean's waves and currents gradually wore away the middle part of the delta, and only a chain of barrier islands now remains.

The river today
Each year, the Mississippi pours more than 500 million tonnes of sand, mud and other sediments into the Gulf of Mexico. Some of these particles have travelled over 3,500 km from the river's source far inland to the north.

The delta of the future?
Winds and ocean currents sweep the sediments southwards from the river's mouth, clouding the water for many kilometres. In thousands of years, this area may become dry land, and the river will have moved on.

NATURE'S SCULPTURES

Rocks may seem hard and unbreakable to us. But even "solid rock" is no match for the forces of nature. Wind picks up sand grains and other particles and hurls them against a rock, sandblasting grooves and cracks in its surface. The sun beats down by day, making the rock expand; during chilly nights, it cools and shrinks. This makes a thousand tiny cracks in the rock's surface.

Rain beats down, getting into the grooves and cracks and weakening the rock. Floodwaters and rivers scour its surface. The chemicals that water absorbs from the air and soil turn it into a very weak acid, which slowly dissolves away certain types of rock, such as limestone.

When water freezes into ice, it expands with considerable force. Water freezing in the grooves and cracks of the rock splits and splinters it. And those rivers of ice, glaciers (page 46), carve away great valleys. All these forces of erosion wear down even the hardest rocks.

Shaped in stone
Striking rock formations around the Earth (but shown here together) have been carved by the forces of erosion. Some types of rocks are much harder and more resistant than others. As the softer, weaker rocks around them are worn away, the tougher rocks remain as weird and wonderful shapes – nature's sculptures.

Elephants in the desert
In the Sahara Desert, sandstones 420 million years old have been cracked and chipped by erosion into the huge cliffs of Tassili n'Ajjer. Cave paintings 7,000 years old depict elephants and antelopes, showing that grass and trees covered the area at that time.

Giant's pebbles
The Harz Mountains, on the old border between the former West and East Germany, were once granite rocks far below the surface. Many cycles of erosion and uplifting have brought them to the surface. Boulders as big as houses lie jumbled like pebbles dropped by a giant.

Valle de la Luna
In northern Argentina, in the foothills of the Andes, is the dry, desolate "Valley of the Moon". Rock columns have been chiselled by windblown sand. Yet fossils in the area show it was once moist and inhabited by giant ferns, lizards and snakes.

A tall old man
The Old Man of Hoy is a thin pencil of rock, 137 metres tall, in the sea near the Orkney Islands. Made of extra-hard sandstone, it was once part of a long cliff that was worn away by the sea.

Smoothed by rain
Heavy monsoon rains have helped to erode the Western Ghats, a mountain chain in western India. Here, a tough cap of rock is an ''umbrella'' to the rain-smoothed cone beneath.

The great bear
In northern Sardinia is a granite headland that has been eroded by – dew! Dew settles in the night and chemically attacks the rock, lingering longer in the shadier places before the Sun dries it. Flakes of rock are loosened and blown away, forming bowl-shaped hollows. This rock is called *Capo d'Orso*, the ''Cape of the Bear''. Can you see why?

City of stone
Ciudad Encantada, the ''Enchanted City'', is near Madrid in Spain. But these bizarre rocky outcrops are not the work of man. Over centuries, hard dolomite slabs have protected portions of the lower limestone from chemical erosion by rainwater (page 44), creating stone ''skyscrapers''.

43

THE WORLD UNDER OUR FEET

Caves have sheltered people for thousands of years. In 1940, near Lascaux in south-west France, four children were searching for their lost dog. They discovered a large cave. On its walls were beautiful paintings of deer, horses, bears and other animals. The cave paintings of Lascaux are now world-famous. They were the first paintings made by people – the cave-dwelling Cro-Magnons – about 17,000 years ago.

How were the caves created in the first place? Most of them are made in limestone rocks, by a simple chemical reaction between the rain, the air and the minerals of the rock. As rainwater seeps through the soil, it absorbs carbon dioxide gas, which turns it into a very weak acid, called *carbonic acid*. This will erode the limestone it comes into contact with. Over thousands of years, as rainwater repeatedly trickles into cracks and holes in the rock the acid erodes them, making them larger and larger. Underground streams wear away the limestone, and thinned patches of rock collapse until, gradually, a system of caves and tunnels is created. Some caves are truly enormous. The world's biggest single cave is Sarawak Chamber in Borneo, which is so large it could house 800 tennis courts.

Cave country

Under the surface of limestone country there may be huge caverns, rushing streams and rivers and endless underground passages eroded into fantastic shapes. The only signs on the surface might be a few small holes, formed where caves below had such thin roofs that they collapsed. The holes provide entrances into the caves for water, animals and adventurous explorers (cavers).

In the beginning
A large cave system develops over centuries. It begins when sedimentary limestone cracks slightly during earth movements, to form small cracks and pockets. Rainwater, drawn ever downwards by gravity, seeps into each tiny crevice, wearing away the rock and enlarging the crevices.

Pavements of rock
In many limestone areas, rainwater quickly seeps underground or forms streams that disappear down holes. Endless erosion and lack of water give rise to dry, rocky, barren land where few plants can grow. The rock erodes along joint lines to produce "limestone pavements".

Swallowed up
Streams plunge down *swallow holes* to the caves below. The water carries some nutrients in it, and these might be enough to feed bizarre, blind, pale, cave-dwelling creatures such as fish, shrimps and salamanders.

Growing up
Carrot-shaped stalagmites grow up where water drips onto the ground (stala*g*mite = *g*round). Like stalactites, they grow on average about one to two millimetres each year, up to about 2 or more metres high.

44

River run dry
Centuries ago, a rushing stream made this tunnel. Then the land rose, or the water level fell, or the river found another route. Now it is dry – an abandoned gallery.

Gone to pot
Once, a stream poured down this hole into the darkness below. Erosion and tilting of the land have diverted the water, and it is now a dry *pot hole*.

Underground "icicles"
As water seeps through the roof of the cave, each drip leaves a tiny portion of its dissolved minerals. These build downwards to form a hanging, icicle-shaped stalactite (stala*c*tite = *c*eiling).

Carry on eroding
The underground river's present course brings it gushing from a rock face about one kilometre away. But in another few centuries this tunnel could be dry, and the river will have eroded its way down to yet another level.

45

THE FROZEN LANDSCAPE

Did you know that ice covers more than one-tenth of the Earth's land area? It is formed as snow falls and gets squashed under its own weight, or as it thaws and re-freezes. Of course, ice only forms where temperatures are below zero – in the polar regions – or high up in the mountains. Almost the entire continent of Antarctica, at the South Pole, is under a blanket of ice one and a half times the size of the USA and more than 4,000 metres thick in places. Three-quarters of our planet's freshwater is locked up as ice covering the land.

Great snowfields in the highest mountains of the world feed thousands of massive glaciers, "rivers of ice", that flow very slowly downhill. The rocks frozen in the base and sides of a glacier can hollow out a mountainside, polish the rocks and even transport underneath it immense boulders weighing hundreds of tonnes. In former times, the biggest glaciers carved away parts of our landscape, that are now warmer and ice-free, into giant valleys.

The hidden ice at sea

An iceberg is a huge block of freshwater ice that has floated off from the end of a glacier into a lake or the sea. It is much bigger than it looks – only about one-sixth of its bulk shows above the water's surface.

Block iceberg

Rounded iceberg

The massive "rivers of ice"

A bird's eye view of a glacier shows how this vast conveyor belt of ice changes the landscape. A glacier slides along, on average, at about one metre each day, but a few, especially in Canada, flow at 25 metres or more per day. The longest glacier in the world, 400 km in length, is in Antarctica.

The glacier's snout

The lower end, or "snout", of the glacier may be on land, or in a lake or sea. Here it is a lot warmer, and the ice melts at the same rate as it flows down-hill, forming a stream of icy water.

On the retreat
This glacier is getting smaller as it melts slightly faster than it is fed. Boulders made of rock, called *erratics*, carried down by the glacier, indicate areas once covered by ice.

Big cracks in the ice
As the brittle ice flows round a sharp bend or over a ridge, it splits to form deep wedge-shaped cracks, called *crevasses*. Some are enormous – 50 metres deep and hundreds of metres long.

The rubble on the sides
The moving ice rubs, rasps and cracks the rock below, picking up bits of stone and boulders. These collect in mounds, known as *lateral moraines*, along the glacier's sides.

Ice-sculpted landscapes
Millions of years ago, glaciers in many parts of the world wore away U-shaped valleys like the Yosemite Valley in the USA. Smaller valleys that open high on the sides of the main one are called *hanging valleys*. Ice may also gouge away the sides of a mountain to form a pointed peak and sharp ridges (*aretes*), as on Mount Fitzroy in Patagonia.

Yosemite Valley

Mount Fitzroy

SEAS, TIDES AND BEACHES

When most of us go to the seaside for our summer holidays, the skies are blue and the sea laps gently on the beach. But the same place in a winter's storm can look very different. The coastline becomes a battleground. Huge waves crash on the shore, hurling themselves against cliffs and rocks with colossal force and carrying away the broken fragments. Air does more damage than the water. Trapped by an incoming wave against the rock face, it is forced at high pressure into every nook and cranny of the rocks, eventually cracking and splitting it. In many places the sea relentlessly erodes the land and ocean currents sweep away the debris. In other places, such as deltas (page 40), the land is winning. As the elements battle it out, the line between land and sea shifts and changes. Over the centuries, cliffs are eaten away and sometimes whole villages and coastal towns are gradually swallowed up by the sea. Channels are blocked by fallen rocks and sandbars form offshore. Maps and charts of coastal waters must be constantly updated, so that sailors do not run their boats aground.

Undercut and overhang
Sea cliffs are one of the best places to see how certain rocks were formed in layers. Storms and high tides undercut the lower cliff, and eventually the overhang crashes down as a pile of rubble.

Rolled by ocean rollers
Waves relentlessly roll rocks and boulders to and fro on the shore. Gradually they are broken and worn into smaller pebbles, and over hundreds of years into tiny particles called sand.

Sorted by size
In this area, wind and waves have swept small sand grains from this area. But they are not strong enough to move larger, heavier boulders and pebbles. This process is called *sorting*.

Refreshed twice daily
Hollows and holes in the rocks fill with sea water to make rockpools. The water is refreshed at every high tide, bringing in floating bits of food and an ever-changing assortment of plants and animals.

Sea shells on the seashore
Hard, limy shells of sea animals are washed up on the shore and slowly broken into fragments, forming shelly sand.

On the beach

The shore is a fascinating example of erosion in action. Most beach sand has been brought from inland by rivers and swept along the coast by water currents. Some comes from erosion of the cliffs behind. Quartz is the most common mineral in sand grains, made from eroded rocks like granite.

Erosion slowdown

To slow erosion, *groynes* (breakwaters) are built into the sea. They break up waves, lessen sideways currents and reduce windblown sand. They also shelter seaweeds, limpets, barnacles and other types of seashore life.

Tied to the tide

Each day the sea level rises and falls, then rises and falls again (due to the gravitational pull of the Moon and the Sun, page 10). The average time between one high tide and the next is 12 hours 25 minutes. The difference in height can be over 10 metres.

Tide flowing (coming in)

Tide ebbing (going out)

At the back of the beach

Winds blow sand grains inland to form dunes. Most plants find it difficult to get a roothold in the shifting grains, but a few, like marram grass, are able to bind the sand and gradually stabilize the dunes.

Wind
Current

Ocean currents

The Earth's rotation, its temperature zones and its wind patterns help to create giant ocean currents that circulate around the globe. These ocean currents affect climate. For example, the warm waters of the Caribbean flow to Northern Europe, creating mild winters.

49

THE LIVING ROCKS IN THE OCEANS

Which tiny animals have over thousands of years built rocks in the oceans so huge that they can be seen from the Moon? Corals have. Each coral is a tiny anemone-like sea creature about two or three millimetres across. As it grows, it builds a minute cup-shaped skeleton to protect the lower part of its jelly-like body, into which it can draw its tentacles for safety. The skeleton is made of calcium carbonate minerals that the coral obtains from sea water. Thousands of corals, packed side by side, grow and their skeletons join together. When they die, more corals grow on top of them. Over many, many years the millions of skeletons combine with sand and other fragments of matter to form a limestone rock, called a coral reef. The world's largest coral reef is the Great Barrier Reef off the coast of Australia; it is over 2,000 km long.

The rich life of the reef

Most corals grow in the warm shallow seas of the tropics, where the water temperature is about 23° to 27°C. You find most of the reefs in the Caribbean and in the Indo-Pacific oceans. The caves, cracks and underhangs in the coral reef are rich feeding grounds for a dazzling variety of fishes, crabs, shellfish and other kinds of sea life, including sharks. The corals themselves are equally dazzling – and come in a myriad types and colours.

Where corals grow

Corals live in shallow, sunny water. They usually grow best on the wind-ward, more exposed, side of a reef. Here the crashing waves aerate the water and prevent mud from suffocating the coral.

Seaweeds and algae

Leeward side

Coral growing on windward side

Bubble coral

This type of coral grows in rounded bubble-like shapes. Like other corals, the tiny coral creatures come out only at night. They wave their tentacles in the sea water, stinging and eating any micro-scopic floating plants and animals they can catch.

Brain coral

This coral has a wavy-surface shape that looks like the human brain – hence its name! In life, coral is covered with a shiny layer of living tissue that shimmers in many colours. After death, only the whitish skeleton remains.

Hard coral

The skeletons of hard corals build up into low, flattened lumps of limestone. But not all corals make reefs. Some grow alone, like tiny sea anemones, lying on the sea bed or stuck to rocks.

Coral colours
The colours of corals are due partly to microscopic plants that are called *zooxanthellae*. These single-celled relatives of seaweeds actually live within the coral's body.

Gorgonian sea fans
These corals grow in beautiful branching patterns. The group includes the red coral which has been used to make jewellery since ancient times.

Bottlebrush coral

How corals grow
The *zooxanthellae* inside the coral's body provide it with food, in return for a place to live. But they need sunlight, which is why corals grow only in shallow water.

Soft coral tree
The "soft corals" are supported mainly by tiny hard spikes within their bodies. They grow into branching, rubbery shapes rather than hard and stony ones.

Groups of coral
Each tiny coral creature is called a *polyp*. The polyps grow together in groups called *colonies*. It is the colony that makes up each branching piece of coral, as shown here.

Ridge coral
This type grows on its side, looking like plates stuck side-on into the sea bed. Many fish, shrimps and other creatures find shelter among the ridges.

51

EARTH'S MYSTERIES

In olden times, an eclipse of the Sun (opposite) struck terror into hearts across the world. The ancient Chinese and Babylonians could predict the movements of the Sun and the phases of the Moon. Yet they had no idea how the Solar System operated (see pages 8–11). When the Moon passed between the Earth and the Sun, eclipsing its light and warmth briefly, the ancient peoples thought it was a sign of the wrath of their god.

Nowadays, science can explain many of the strange happenings on our planet. And we know that forces far away in space affect what happens here on Earth. For instance, the Northern and

Southern Lights are vast moving curtains of light in the night sky towards the poles. People wondered why they brighten every 27 days or so, and then fade. Satellites and telescopes have helped to explain. The lights are electrical discharges, like those in a fluorescent striplight. They are formed when gases high in the atmosphere are hit by the "solar wind" – high-speed particles shot out from *sunspots* on the Sun. The Sun spins every 27 days, and the particles shoot out from its sunspots like the light beam from a lighthouse's rotating mirror. They "shine" on Earth every 27 days and illuminate the fabulous display of the polar lights.

Worldwide wonders
These strange happenings from around the world puzzled people for centuries, but now they can be explained by modern scientific knowledge. Yet there are still many important natural phenomena for earth scientists to explore, such as how to predict weather patterns and earthquakes more accurately.

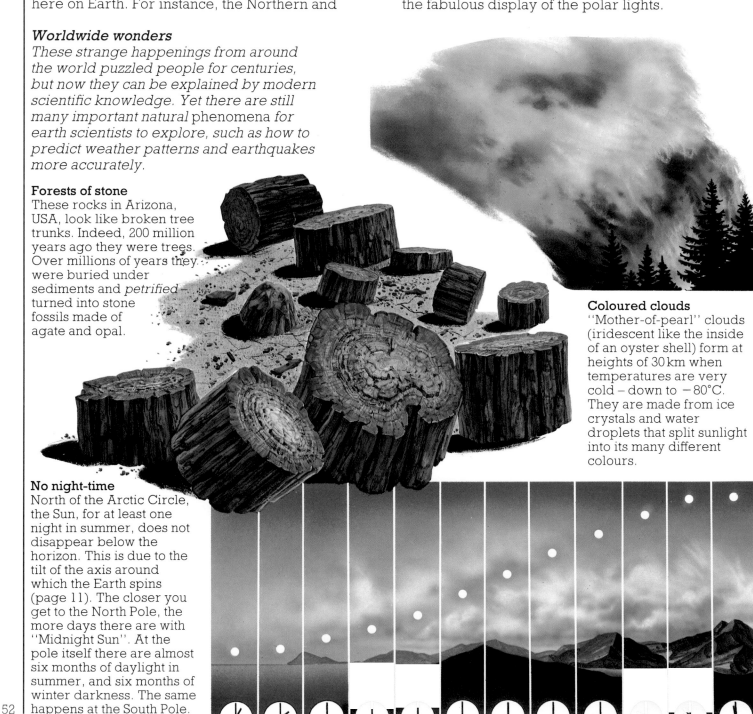

Forests of stone
These rocks in Arizona, USA, look like broken tree trunks. Indeed, 200 million years ago they were trees. Over millions of years they were buried under sediments and *petrified* – turned into stone fossils made of agate and opal.

Coloured clouds
"Mother-of-pearl" clouds (iridescent like the inside of an oyster shell) form at heights of 30 km when temperatures are very cold – down to −80°C. They are made from ice crystals and water droplets that split sunlight into its many different colours.

No night-time
North of the Arctic Circle, the Sun, for at least one night in summer, does not disappear below the horizon. This is due to the tilt of the axis around which the Earth spins (page 11). The closer you get to the North Pole, the more days there are with "Midnight Sun". At the pole itself there are almost six months of daylight in summer, and six months of winter darkness. The same happens at the South Pole.

Now you see it . . .
A mirage is something which appears to be there, but is really elsewhere. Some mirages are formed because light, bent by warm air near the ground, reaches an observer hundreds of kilometres distant – yet appears to be near by.

Observer

Warm air

Mirage

Cold air

Solar eclipse
As the Moon goes round the Earth, and the Earth goes round the Sun, the Moon occasionally passes in front of the Sun and temporarily blots out the light (*eclipses*).

Earth

Sun

Moon

Curtains of lights
Every 27 days or so, colours glow in the night skies near the poles. The base of the "curtain" is about 100 km high, and the top may be more than 300 km in altitude. Their brightness varies from year to year.

Northern lights
(*Aurora borealis*)

Southern lights
(*Aurora australis*)

It's snowing in the desert!
Freak strong, cold winds high in the atmosphere can bring snow over usually hot deserts. The snow settles on the desert sands and plants. However it soon melts, and soaks in or is dried out by the Sun.

Big Moon, small Moon
Photographs show that the Moon is "bigger" at some times of the month. This is because the orbit of the Moon around the Earth is not a circle, but an *ellipse*. When the Moon is closer to us, it looks larger than usual in the sky.

53

NATURAL RESOURCES

From the Earth's crust come the natural resources on which our modern world depends. Oil (petroleum), coal and natural gas provide energy. Metals such as iron (for steel) and aluminium are used to make planes, trains and road vehicles, and for machines of all kinds. Sand, stone and clay make our buildings. We use lots of other natural substances, from the sulphur that hardens rubber for car tyres to the silicon made into computer "chips".

Of all the Earth's resources oil is probably the most widely used and the most valuable. It has formed from the bodies of tiny floating plants and animals that settled on the sea bed, over millions of years. Oil straight from the well is thick, dark and gooey, known as "crude". But after separation into its various constituents at a *refinery*, it is used to make an almost endless list of substances, fuel in the form of petrol, diesel and kerosene (for planes), oil for power stations, lubricating oils, waxes and solvents and even hard materials – synthetic fibres, detergents, plastics of all kinds – as well as the inks on this page!

Drilling rig
The oil in a newly drilled well usually comes to the surface under natural pressure. Later, it has to be pumped up. The massive drill comes in sections and is hoisted by a crane into its housing, called a *derrick*.

A fortune under the sea bed
Oil is found under the land and the ocean, in sedimentary rocks that were once part of the sea bed (see page 26). There are around 700 oil rigs dotted about the Earth's oceans. Some are test drilling to discover new oil and gas fields. Others, the production rigs, extract the oil and gas, and feed it to the shore by pipeline or tanker.

Helipad

Lots of bores
A drilling rig bores up to a dozen holes into the oil "bubble" deep below. This helps to equalize the pressure in different parts of the oilfield and gives a more even flow.

Manifold

Oil production
Oil is inflammable, and drilling for it is risky. A *manifold* on the sea bed controls the pressure and stops oil spurting into the sea. A *flare stack* burns off the surplus gases in the oil. The crew live and work on the production platform, and the men and supplies are ferried in and out by helicopter.

Ready-made or ore?

Some of the Earth's resources, such as coal, are mined "ready-made" for us to use. But most metals occur mixed up with minerals and other substances in rocks. An *ore* is a rock that contains enough of a valuable substance (usually a metal) to be worth mining. Some iron ores are two-thirds iron, but most copper ores are only one or two per cent copper. The less concentrated a substance, the more ore that must be mined. A "rich" vein of gold ore yields only 20 grams of gold for each tonne of rock!

Copper

Gold

Silver

Lead

Coal

Haematite (iron ore)

Flare stack burns off excess gases

Tanking up with oil

The oil tankers that take away the crude oil are the largest of all ships. Some carry more than 300,000 tonnes of oil and are almost half a kilometre long. It takes about six minutes to walk from one end of the tanker to the other.

Main storage tanks

Loading buoy

Giant steel tanks moored to the sea bed hold oil ready for pumping into the tanker. There is no likelihood of them sinking – oil floats on water! Platforms near land pump their oil ashore along pipelines.

55

EARTH'S TREASURE CHEST

"Beauty is in the eye of the beholder". If enough beholders think that something is beautiful, and it is in short supply, then it tends to be valuable as well. Gemstones are naturally occurring minerals that are valuable because of their natural beauty, durability and rarity, and the way they are cut and polished (see below). Each gemstone has a characteristic pattern of cuts, to produce tiny flat faces, called *facets*. Each facet is at a slight angle to the others, so that light is reflected again and again to give each gem its characteristic sparkle.

There are about 3,000 different kinds of minerals in the Earth's crust. Only a hundred or so have exciting colours, patterning and sparkle, and could be called gemstones, and of these, only 15 or 20 are commonly used for jewellery, ornaments and sculptures. The first stage is to mine the gem-containing rock. Most gems are rare, and many tonnes of rock must be sorted to obtain gems worth keeping. In a diamond mine, 25 tonnes of rock yield one gram of diamonds, and most of these are almost too small to see. The second stage is cutting and polishing the gem from its rough, natural state, so that its colour, sheen and sparkle are shown to best effect. Some gemstones are valuable for practical purposes as well. Diamonds and garnets are so hard that they are used in industry for cutting tools.

A priceless collection

Most of the gems shown here have been formed in the Earth over millions of years by the same enormous pressures and temperatures that have created the rocks around them. However, pearls, amber, ivory and other substances formed by living things are technically not gems.

Amber (*left*)
The ancient Greeks thought that amber was the hardened rays of a sunset. In fact it is fossilized sap, or resin, from coniferous trees which grew millions of years ago.

Insect trapped in amber

Agate (*above*)
This is a form of quartz. It is created when gas bubbles trapped in molten rock slowly fill with layers of quartz, coloured by traces of iron and other elements.

Tourmaline (*above*)
Tourmaline, the birthstone for October, forms as slender crystals with three, six or nine sides. It may be almost any colour, from colourless to glossy black.

Jade (*above*)
Polished jade has a glassy look and a warm colour, usually mottled green. It has been carved since ancient times by many peoples, especially the Chinese, into sculptures, ornaments, knives and other tools.

Cut quartz

The commonest mineral
Quartz (silicon dioxide) is the most abundant mineral on Earth. But only rarely does it form transparent, colourless crystals that have value as gems.

Turquoise (*above*)
Opaque rather than clear, and a beautiful brilliant blue or blue-green in colour, these stones are usually cut and polished into rounded egg shapes.

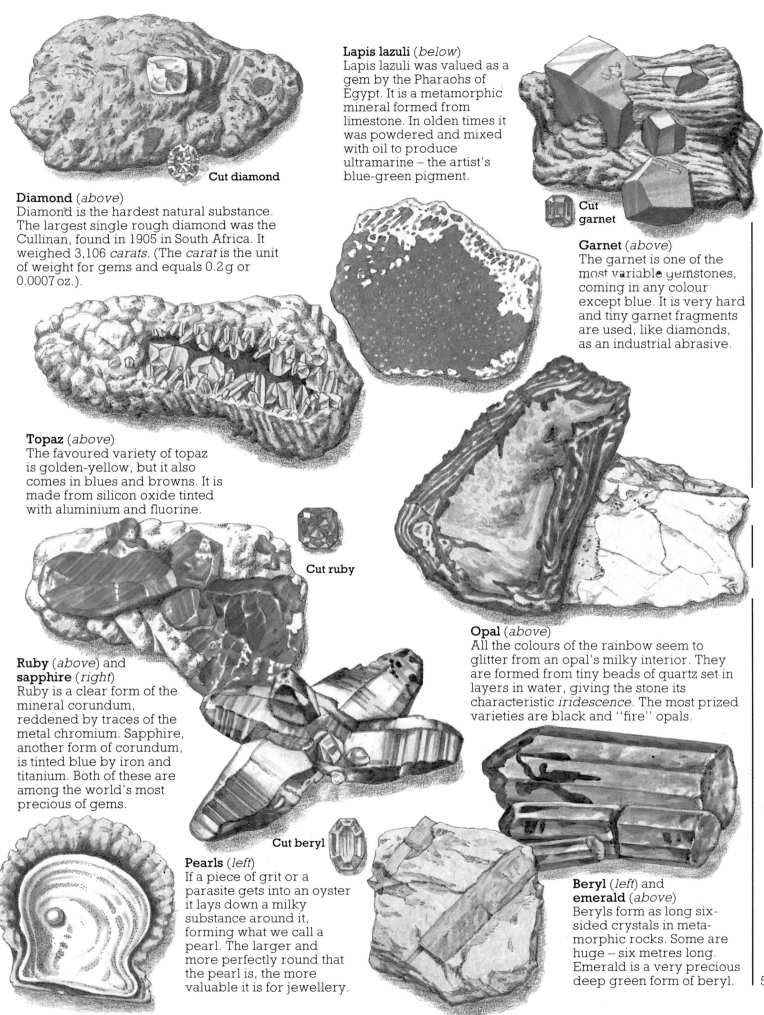

Lapis lazuli (*below*)
Lapis lazuli was valued as a gem by the Pharaohs of Egypt. It is a metamorphic mineral formed from limestone. In olden times it was powdered and mixed with oil to produce ultramarine – the artist's blue-green pigment.

Cut diamond

Cut garnet

Diamond (*above*)
Diamond is the hardest natural substance. The largest single rough diamond was the Cullinan, found in 1905 in South Africa. It weighed 3,106 *carats*. (The *carat* is the unit of weight for gems and equals 0.2 g or 0.0007 oz.).

Garnet (*above*)
The garnet is one of the most variable gemstones, coming in any colour except blue. It is very hard and tiny garnet fragments are used, like diamonds, as an industrial abrasive.

Topaz (*above*)
The favoured variety of topaz is golden-yellow, but it also comes in blues and browns. It is made from silicon oxide tinted with aluminium and fluorine.

Cut ruby

Opal (*above*)
All the colours of the rainbow seem to glitter from an opal's milky interior. They are formed from tiny beads of quartz set in layers in water, giving the stone its characteristic *iridescence*. The most prized varieties are black and "fire" opals.

Ruby (*above*) and **sapphire** (*right*)
Ruby is a clear form of the mineral corundum, reddened by traces of the metal chromium. Sapphire, another form of corundum, is tinted blue by iron and titanium. Both of these are among the world's most precious of gems.

Cut beryl

Pearls (*left*)
If a piece of grit or a parasite gets into an oyster it lays down a milky substance around it, forming what we call a pearl. The larger and more perfectly round that the pearl is, the more valuable it is for jewellery.

Beryl (*left*) and **emerald** (*above*)
Beryls form as long six-sided crystals in metamorphic rocks. Some are huge – six metres long. Emerald is a very precious deep green form of beryl.

POLLUTION OF THE PLANET

In today's overcrowded world, more and more of the Earth's natural resources are being used up. Although steps are being taken to control many forms of pollution, scientists and conservationsts are particularly worried about:

Acid rain (see below) The great pine forests of northern Europe and northern Canada are decaying and dying from the effects of acid rain, originating in industrial regions hundreds of kilometres away.

The greenhouse effect Burning petrol, coal, forests or anything else creates the gas, carbon dioxide. Its amounts are slowly building up, and scientists predict that the extra carbon dioxide will trap the Sun's warmth in the atmosphere, in the same way that glass traps warmth in a greenhouse. Gradually the Earth's temperature will rise, with disastrous effects on climate, wildlife and crops.

Radioactive pollution Nuclear power stations make cheap electricity and save valuable natural fuels, but the problem is how to dispose of the radioactive waste without future hazard.

Scarring the landscape
Where coal, metal ores, gemstones, gravel, building stones and other valuable substances occur near the surface, great quarries and *open-cast* mines are dug to extract them. Fortunately, these days, most areas are re-landscaped by the mining and quarrying companies.

Blowing in the wind
Fertilizers, weedkillers and pesticides are used by farmers to produce bigger yields from the crops. But the chemicals affect other plants, and animals as well, seeping into the ground and polluting rivers and streams.

Undisposable disposables
Our modern society throws away endless ''disposable'' packages, containers, old furniture, beds, cars, machinery ... Some of this will rot down when buried, but plastics, especially, do not. They pile up and will pollute the planet for hundreds of years to come unless a means of dissolving them is found.

The cost for the Earth
Each town has its factories, power stations, rubbish dumps and sewage works. They are part of modern life, giving us the lifestyle and luxuries we take for granted. But there are many thousands of such towns around the Earth. How long can our planet cope with the pollution they produce?

Oil all gone
Fuel made from oil (petroleum), which took millions of years to form, will be guzzled up in a century at the present rate of use. Exhaust fumes from cars and trucks contain chemicals that help to create acid rain (right) and, in sunlight, make suffocating smog.

What goes up . . .
Fumes from vehicles, power stations and factories dissolve in the water droplets of clouds, to make sulphuric acid. This falls back to Earth, perhaps hundreds of kilometres away, as *acid rain* that kills trees, fish and other wildlife.

Oil on troubled waters
Supertankers carry thousands of tonnes of oil from the oilfields to the industrial countries that use it. Accidental leaks and spillages are bound to occur, and oil slicks kill seabirds and shore life.

Wasted warmth
Smoke from power stations is a major cause of acid rain (left). Many stations are inefficient, giving off vast amounts of heat as steam from huge cooling towers, when it could be used to warm local homes and buildings.

Dirty water
Sewage, chemicals and other wastes wash into rivers and eventually into the sea. If they are not treated properly they kill fish and water life, and carry diseases downstream to people who use the water.

The nuclear threat
An accident at a nuclear power station, or firing a nuclear weapon, could release invisible but deadly *radioactivity*. This would kill all life nearby, and cause illness and suffering many hundreds of kilometres away.

Conservation and recycling
The Earth's oil, coal, gas and other natural substances will run out unless we find better, more efficient ways to make the things our modern society wants. Electric power can be generated from hot rocks deep underground or by light and heat from the Sun (page 60). Metals, glass, paper and other substances can be used again (*recycled*) to conserve resources.

Rechargeable electric vehicle

Solar-powered car

Geothermal power

Recyclable products

Glass bottles

Waste vegetables

Metal cans   Paper and packaging

Factories and industries
Industrial processes use enormous quantities of raw materials and power, and produce polluting smoke and by-products as well as their goods.

Pollution takes off
Every minute, high above the ground, aircraft burn tonnes of kerosene – made from irreplaceable petroleum. Their jets pour out fumes and unburned fuel, which may damage the upper atmosphere.

59

NATURAL POWER

Our major energy sources today – coal, oil, natural gas – will not last for ever. The search is on for alternative forms of energy which are less polluting and which will last as long as the Earth itself. Hydro-electric dams, that harness the energy of moving water, are already in use in many countries. Harnessing tidal power is another possibility. A tidal power station on the Rance River, in northern France, generates 240 megawatts of electricty, enough to supply a small town. In fact most natural power schemes are designed to turn their energy source into electricity. This is because electricity can be carried by cables, conveniently, silently and without pollution, to wherever it is needed. Other forms of natural power – the tides, the wind, the sun, for example – are only suitable for places with high tides, or strong, consistent winds, or plenty of sunshine. But covering a beautiful hillside with *solar cells* or windmills does tend to mar the landscape and the whirring windmill blades create "noise pollution".

Circling sails
Windmills, a familiar sight two or three centuries ago, are used for various jobs, such as grinding wheat to make flour. Then power from coal and oil replaced the wind, and many windmills fell into disuse and disrepair.

Windmills of the future?
Wind power may be one answer to our energy needs for the future. These modern windmills, tall as a 10-storey building, were designed by computer and built from lightweight metals and carbon-fibre. Their power is used to generate electricity.

The ultimate energy source
The power-producing devices shown here each depend, in the end, on the Sun. Some use its light or heat directly. Others rely on winds, which are air movements caused by the Sun warming different parts of the atmosphere as the Earth rotates. Even falling water is Sun-powered, since the Sun evaporated it from the sea, to form clouds and fall as rain.

Solar power
The Sun's light energy can be turned into electricity by solar cells. Or its heat energy can be focused by hundreds of mirrors into one spot, to boil water that turns into steam, that in turn drives an electricity-generating turbine.

Falling water
A waterwheel turns because gravity pulls water downwards over it. Old waterwheels turned mill stones or pumped water to irrigate crops. Today rushing water spins turbine blades that generate electricity in the hydro-electric power station.

Hanging around
In the right weather, a hang-glider pilot can gain height by circling in a *thermal*, a column of rising warm air. In this way the pilot can fly for many kilometres – using no fuel.

The solar plane
In this experimental plane-cum-glider *solar cells* convert light into electricity that drives an electric motor, which turns the propellor. But when the Sun goes in, the plane glides back down to the ground!

The wind farm
In California, USA, several thousand windmills line a particularly windy valley and generate enough electricity to power 100,000 homes. Medium-sized windmills like these (the blades are 45 metres across) are cheaper and easier to make than a few giant windmills producing the same amount of power.

The new age of sail
Several cargo ships have recently been fitted with specially designed sails. The sails are folded in half when the wind drops. Operated by computer, the sail power and engine power are combined in the most efficient way, with great savings in fuel costs.

GLOSSARY

(Words in *italics* have their own entries in the glossary.)

acid rain
Rain that has absorbed acidic gases in the air, damaging rocks and life.

asthenosphere
The part of the earth's *mantle* immediately below the lithosphere made of hot, molten rock.

atmosphere
The mixture of gases, clouds and dust in the layer of "air" around the Earth.

axis
An imaginary line through the Earth, on which the planet turns once each day like a wheel turning on an axle.

calcite
A clear or white *mineral* made from pure *calcium carbonate*.

calcium carbonate
A chemical molecule made of calcium, carbon and oxygen ($CaCO_3$), found in *calcite*, chalk and other *limestones*.

carbon dioxide
A colourless, odourless gas (CO_2) that makes up 1/3,000th of the *atmosphere*.

carbonic acid
The weak acid formed when water absorbs *carbon dioxide* gas from the *atmosphere* or the soil.

chromium
A natural chemical found in some *minerals*, such as rubies, that affects their colour.

climate
The average weather conditions in an area over a long period of time.

condensation
When air cools, and water vapour (a gas) turns into liquid water (the opposite of *evaporation*).

continent
One of the very large land masses on Earth, e.g. Africa or Australia.

core
The innermost part of the Earth, partly solid and partly liquid.

corundum
A very hard *mineral* (aluminium and oxygen – Al_2O_3), sometimes found in the form of gems such as ruby.

crust
The relatively thin outer layer of the Earth. Under the crust is the *mantle*.

currents, ocean
Large-scale movements of sea water, resulting from the upper sea layers being heated by the Sun and the rotation of the Earth.

delta
The area of flat land, often triangle-shaped, through which a river runs into the sea (see also *estuary*).

equator
An imaginary line exactly halfway between North and South poles, at right angles to the *axis*.

erosion
The gradual wearing away of the Earth's surface by rain, wind, ice and so on.

estuary
Where a river widens out at its mouth and flows into the sea (see also *delta*).

evaporation
When water turns from being a liquid into a gas – water vapour (the opposite of *condensation*).

fluorine
A natural chemical found in some *minerals*, such as topaz, that affects their colour.

geothermal
Heat from under the Earth's surface.

granite
A hard *igneous* rock made of three main *minerals*, mostly *quartz* and feldspar, with mica or lornblende.

gravitational
To do with gravity, the "pulling force" of any large body such as the Earth.

hydro-electricity
Electricity made using the power of running water to spin a *turbine* and drive a generator.

The Earth mapped out
Shown here are the main continents (large land masses), sub-continents and oceans of the world. Antarctica (the continent surrounding the South Pole) is shown on the small map on the far right. The technique of transferring the Earth's features to a flat sheet of paper is called a *projection*.

igneous
Rock that has heated up, melted and then cooled and solidified.

iridescence
A rainbow-like sheen on an object that changes colour as the light shining on it alters.

limestone
A type of rock containing, among other substances, forms of *calcium carbonate* (lime).

lithospheric plate
One of the giant, curved, slowly moving, jigsaw-like pieces that make up the Earth's surface.

magma
Molten rock far below the ground.

manganese
A natural chemical found in some *minerals*, such as *quartz*, that affects their colour.

magnetic field
The invisible force around an object, such as the Earth, that attracts other objects to it.

manifold
A container built to withstand pressure, as around an *oil* well hole.

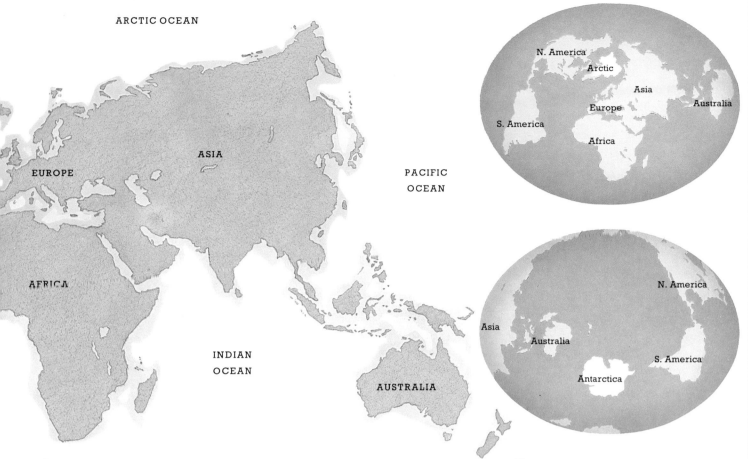

ARCTIC OCEAN

EUROPE

ASIA

AFRICA

INDIAN
OCEAN

PACIFIC
OCEAN

AUSTRALIA

N. America
Arctic
Asia
Europe
Australia
S. America
Africa

Asia
Australia
N. America
Antarctica
S. America

mantle
The middle layer of the Earth, between the *crust* and the *core*.

megawatt
A unit of power, often used for electricity. One megawatt equals one million watts (an ordinary light bulb is about 100 watts).

metamorphic
A type of rock that has been changed but not melted by great heat or pressure.

migration
The movement of animals such as birds or antelopes to another place on the Earth, usually with the seasons.

mineral
A natural, non-living substance with a characteristic chemical make-up. For example, quartz is made from *silicon* and oxygen (silicon dioxide SiO_2). Rocks are mixtures of minerals.

monsoon
The heavy rains that occur seasonally in and around the Indian Ocean.

oil
A naturally occurring fuel just below the Earth's surface – resulting from decayed plants and animals.

ore
A rock or *mineral* from which a valuable substance, such as a metal or gemstone, is obtained.

plankton
Microscopic creatures that drift in oceans, lakes and rivers.

poles
The two opposite ends of the Earth's *axis*; they are known as the North Pole and the South Pole.

quartz
See *mineral*.

reef
An area of rock, mainly *limestone*, in shallow sea water, laid down over centuries by corals.

sandbar
A ridge of sand on the coast, formed by the action of wind, tides and ocean *currents*.

sandstone
A type of rock formed from sand grains cemented together.

sedimentary
A type of rock formed when sediments, particles of sand and silt, collect, making a solid mass.

silicon
A chemical substance that is very common in rocks and forms *minerals* such as quartz.

solar cell
A device that converts light (usually sunlight) into electricity.

sulphur
A common chemical substance. The gas sulphur dioxide dissolves in water in the *atmosphere* to form *acid rain*.

sunspot
A dark spot on the Sun's surface where the temperature is lower than elsewhere.

temperate
Between the *tropical* and the polar regions, where the *climate* is never extreme during the year, rarely very hot or very cold.

tropical
The zone around the Earth's *equator*, about 5,100km wide, where the *climate* is very warm all year.

turbine
A specially designed fan with many blades, spun efficiently by wind, water currents, exhaust gases and so on (see *hydro-electricity*).

INDEX